HEADS UP!

Rob Alcraft

Illustrated by Shahab Shamshirsaz

OXFORD

UNIVERSITY PRESS

Contents

Heads Up!

Would you put a model ship on your head? Would you grow a beard and put a little bag over it at night? Well, it's been done. With headgear and hairstyles, anything goes – as you'll see! This book shows you how people have decorated their heads, taking you from **prehistoric** times to the present day.

WHEN   **WHERE**

24 000 BCE

Europe

This is probably one of the oldest hairstyles you'll ever see, and it still looks neat! Thousands of years ago, this figure was carved out of a tusk from a very hairy animal, a woolly mammoth.

WHEN **8000 BCE** **WHERE** **Syria**

Some of the oldest tools ever found are combs like this one. It means people have been combing their hair for thousands of years – and they still haven't got all the knots out!

WHEN **3100 BCE** **WHERE** **Egypt**

Don't ever moan about having a haircut again. In ancient Egypt, whether you were a boy or a girl, this is what you got. Hair was shaved off all over leaving just a plait on one side.

WHEN **WHERE**

1458 BCE **Egypt**

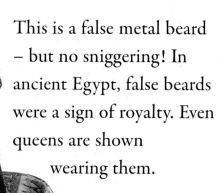

This is a false metal beard – but no sniggering! In ancient Egypt, false beards were a sign of royalty. Even queens are shown wearing them.

WHEN **WHERE**

650 BCE **Greece**

Scared? You should be. This helmet was worn by a warrior. It would have been polished until it shone. Behind all the glinting metal, you would only see the glaring eyes of the man who was trying to kill you. Yikes!

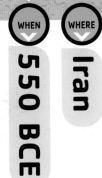

WHEN 550 BCE

WHERE Iran

This soldier from ancient Persia is wearing an early type of turban. Turbans are a cloth that wraps round your head. They are one of the oldest kinds of headgear, and they are still worn today.

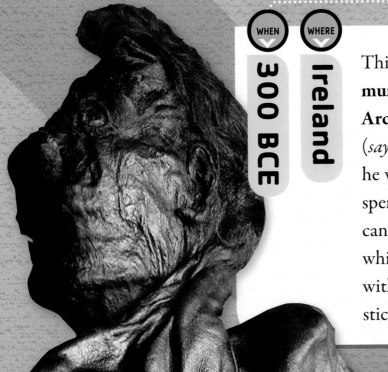

WHEN 300 BCE

WHERE Ireland

This man was found **mummified** in a **peat bog**. **Archaeologists** (*say* ar-kee-ol-o-jists) believe he was murdered. He'd spent time on his hair. We can still see his hairstyle which he had spiked up with gel made from the sticky **resin** of pine trees.

WHEN **WHERE**

73 CE **Italy**

In ancient Rome, you had to keep up with the latest hair fashions – even if you were a statue! Some were made with their own stone wigs which could be swapped when fashions changed.

WHEN

WHERE

200

Nigeria

We don't know much about the ancient Nok people, but we do know that style mattered to them! The Nok made beautiful clay sculptures, carefully modelling fantastic hats and hairstyles like this one.

WHEN

WHERE

668

Europe

If you were a priest or monk in the early Christian church, you had to have this **tonsure** hairstyle. If you felt cold, there was a special hat to keep your bald patch warm.

WHEN

WHERE

850

Nigeria

The lines on this metal head show scars called **ichi**. Scars like these were marks of a leader for the Igbo Ukwu (*say* ee-boa uk-wu) people. Not just anyone was allowed a face like this!

WHEN

WHERE

970

Norway

This helmet probably saved the Viking king who wore it from a very serious headache. It has a dent from a big sword that could have smashed the king's skull.

1050 1100 1150 1200 1250

WHEN WHERE

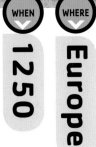

1250

Europe

This is a chaperon. It was a hood that covered your head and shoulders. Chaperons were worn everywhere, in all kinds of ways. They were even worn as a kind of giant piled-up knot – very fashionable!

Do you want to swap?

11

1449

Europe

This is a steeple hat, worn by princesses and rich ladies. Some steeple hats were more than a metre high – making it difficult to get through a door!

1500

South America

The Inca people thought that hair had superpowers. This **headdress** is made of 96 plaits of human hair. It was worn by a priest. The Inca believed it gave him the power to talk to their gods.

WHEN 1514

WHERE England

Even kings look silly sometimes. This helmet was given to England's Henry VIII as a present. Yes, he may actually have worn it.

WHEN 1550

WHERE Mexico

This is the face of Smoking Mirror. He was one of the Aztec people's gods. This mask was worn by a priest or a lord. It looks spooky, and it is! It's made from a human skull.

1570   1580   1590   1600

WHEN **WHERE**

1575

Japan

Samurai warriors used these fierce-looking helmets for protection and to frighten their enemies. It probably worked!

 WHEN **WHERE**

1619

Europe

This creepy costume was invented by a French doctor to protect him from the **plague**. The doctor believed 'bad air' carried the deadly disease. The weird beak was filled with straw and herbs. He thought this would filter the air around him.

14

WHEN

WHERE

1624

Europe and North America

Wigs were in fashion in Europe and America for nearly 200 years. Most men wore them all the time. This is a 'full bottom' wig, but there were short ones and curly ones, and even wigs with pigtails.

WHEN

WHERE

1644

China

Have your hair cut **queue-style**, like this – or have your whole head cut off. This was the choice when the Qing (*say* ching) **dynasty** took power in China. **Barbers** carrying swords helped men to choose.

1698

France and Russia

French lords and kings loved their beards. Some even put little bags over them while they slept, to keep them neat and glossy. However, the Russian ruler, Peter the Great, hated beards. Men with beards had to pay a **tax** or cut them off.

1769

New Zealand

Everything you needed to know about this Maori (*say* mow-ree) man was written on his face. The patterns of scars are called **moko**. They told the story of his family and his life.

WHEN 1778

WHERE France

Yes, that really is a ship on someone's head! This astonishing hairstyle celebrated a French sea victory over the English. At the time people also put models of Paris, whole vegetables and even stuffed animals in their hairstyles.

WHEN 1822

WHERE North America

You wouldn't argue with a man from the Native American Pawnee tribe unless you were looking for trouble. They were famous as warriors and also for this hairstyle. People still wear it – although now it's called a '**Mohican**'.

17

WHEN

1849

WHERE

Worldwide

This might not look like a cowboy's hat – but this **bowler hat** was a favourite in the American Wild West. It was first made for **gamekeepers** in England who kept bashing their heads on trees. Today lots of people still wear bowler hats, including Quechua (*say* ketch-wa) women in Bolivia.

WHEN

1867

WHERE

Japan

In Japan, women decorated their hair with combs called **kanzashi**. There were special kanzashi for each month of the year: blossoms and butterflies in spring and trailing leaves in autumn.

WHEN

 WHERE

1920

Europe and North America

Short hair for women? Outrageous! Most women grew their hair long – until this 'bob' hairstyle appeared. It was new and in the 1920s it was shocking.

WHEN

WHERE

1968

Europe and North America

Long hair for men? Outrageous! Most men and boys wore their hair short, until this long-haired fashion appeared. Hair like this could easily get you sent home from school!

You're looking at the oldest way to dress up – face paint. People have been painting their faces for thousands of years.

NOW

Doesn't this hairstyle look a little like the one carved out of a mammoth tusk thousands of years ago?

In the time between, we've invented the wheel and visited space, but up on our heads, not much has really changed. In ancient times, our hairstyles and headgear said a lot about who we were and where we came from – and they still do today.

We're all part of a fabulous and hairy human story – one that never ends.

It's the latest thing!

It's the latest thing!

21

Glossary

archaeologist: someone who finds remains of ancient places

barber: someone whose job it is to cut men's hair

bowler hat: a hard black hat with a curved brim and round top

dynasty: a series of rulers (such as kings and queens) from the same family

gamekeeper: someone whose job it is to protect birds and animals

headdress: a covering worn on the head for special occasions

ichi: marks carved into the face, worn mainly by men in some parts of Nigeria

Mohican: a haircut where the head is shaved except for a strip of hair down the middle

moko: traditional Maori body and face tattoos

mummified: preserved

peat bog: peat is rotted plant material in a wet ground called a bog

plague: a dangerous illness that can spread quickly

prehistoric: from a long time ago, before written records were kept

queue-style: a hairstyle with a plait of hair worn hanging down behind the back

resin: a sticky substance that comes from some trees and plants

tax: an amount of money that people have to pay to the government

tonsure: the part of a monk or priest's head that has been shaved

Index

About the Author

I'm a dad, and I write books. I work in an old caravan, parked in a field. It's cold in the winter, but it has a lovely view. I don't look at the view though, because I'm too busy writing.

I don't have a lot of hair left, so writing *Heads Up!* was perfect. I got to look at *other* people's hair, and all their fantastic hats – and those funny curly wigs. I think I'm going to get one!

Greg Foot, Series Editor

I've loved science ever since the day I took my papier mâché volcano into school. I filled it with far too much baking powder, vinegar and red food colouring, and WHOOSH! I covered the classroom ceiling in red goo. Now I've got the best job in the world: I present TV shows for the BBC, answer kids' science questions on YouTube, and make huge explosions on stage at festivals!

Working on TreeTops inFact has been great fun. There are so many brilliant books, and guess what ... they're all packed full of awesome facts! What's your favourite?